Thoughts In My Head

Vegas James

BookLeaf Publishing

India | USA | UK

Presentation by *BookLeaf Publishing*

Web: www.bookleafpub.com

E-mail: info@bookleafpub.com

ISBN : 9789357447737

First edition 2021

DEDICATION

To my wife,

My children,

And to you.

ACKNOWLEDGEMENT

To my wife: For not allowing me to give up on my passion, even when I thought it had abandoned me.

To my kids: For giving me reasons to continue to make you proud. Grow old, not up.

To my friends and family for supporting me on my written adventures.

To my inspirations found far and wide, through the arts of literature, music, visual arts, and imagination.

And to Rick, for "allowing me to use whatever he's said in the past for my wanky quote"

PREFACE

This book came to be because of my wife. A year ago, I had written my first book titled "Buried Alive Behind Enemy Lines," which was a passion project more than anything. It was to see if I could write a book, having no prior training on how to do so, and it was a proud moment when I had both finished and self-published it. A few months later, my wife had a terrible accident to which it had come close to taking her life. This took away all of my focus from writing and for a year, I had barely written anything so I could focus on her and our family.

She put me on the spot and said, "I've signed you up to a 21 day writing challenge. You have three weeks to write 21 pieces and you will finish it,"

This is the final product of those 21 days. It wasn't easy, but it rekindled my love for writing and thinking.

A New Beginning

Through a seed,
I was born
I grew
thrived
flourished
only to be cut down in my prime.

They took my corpse
from my birthplace,
defiled
mutilated
taking only what they wanted
and disposed of what remained.

I travelled far and wide
or so it seemed
reunited
along with my brothers
and sisters
who suffered the same fate as I?

As we stopped in our tracks
they dragged us away
plunged us down into the darkness
and fed us to the monsters

to feast on our flesh,
consuming what little we had left within.

I thought this was the end for me
of my journey
the final chapter of my story
until I was reborn
It gave me another chance
to live once more.

Stitched and bound
and tattooed throughout
for you, the reader, to witness
you hold my life within your hands
so I ask you
am I everything you hoped I would be?

Or was my sacrifice made in vain?

A Past Life

The moon is high, the suns arise,
Subliminal consciousness has joined me,
Extracting myself from the worlds within,
Only to partake in the trades of death and greed.

I attach my mask, the one with the smile,
For it may fool the world, but it does not fool the
mirror,
I power on the vessel, this chariot of decay,
For now, it is time to go to work.

Slowly, light eradicates the surrounding
darkness,
Distortion feeds my brain and fuels my body,
It pounds within my skull with flawless rhythm,
But never enough to disguise the slavery.

Carting the corpses of those with no choice,
Body bags and box coffins shared with their
brethren,
They'll consume the flesh and bury the evidence,
Trading one's life for another.

At day's end, when all hope seems lost,
I am rewarded sparingly for my efforts,

Before washing away the victims in my soul,
And to fall back into the abyss once more.

Ash

The thing I struggle with most with writing
Is that I want it to be perfect!
I want it to hit the metaphorical sweet spot
If you know what I mean,
I want to make you think
Make you feel
I want to find a way
To move you somehow.

Sometimes it's possible
Other times, it's not.

And then there's you.

Writing about you
Is the hardest
It's not because I can't
It's because I love you
And no matter how hard I try,
To find the perfect words for you
They never feel as if they can bear the weight
To the incredible
And beautiful woman
that you are.

So, I'll continue my quest,
In search of the perfect piece of literature
Throughout this world,
And beyond
Until then,
I leave you with this.

I love that you're my human.

Asthmatic Equilibrium

My inspiration's suffocating
Like a flame craving oxygen,
It struggles to breathe
An asthmatic equilibrium
The inhaler reads, "Failure"
Must be foreign for something
Tasting of old memories
And that timc I almost lost you.

I don't know why,
But I cannot stop breathing it in.

Broken

It feels like it never stops raining
Falling from the heavens,
Found within the raindrops,
Emotional torment,
Within the air surrounding them,
You must understand
The rain will stop when it's time.

The coven weeps for you
When your soul feels like this,
Your brothers and sisters,
Ache for you
With you,
When you ache,
But love
You'll never go without.

The moon will forever shine for you
Even when it's dark
It's only reminding you that things will shine
once again
As long as you'll allow it to.

The earth feels your pain,

But doesn't understand it
It can never feel what you feel
Witness what you've witnessed
Embrace what you've embraced
And it doesn't understand how grateful it is
To have been within your presence
At the best,
And worst of times
But it feels your pain.

It looks forward to the day
When it may embrace you longer than anyone
else.
It should consider itself lucky.
The spirits are with you on your journey
From here to there
And us mortal beings are here for you
When the spirits seem distant
Never give up
For we won't allow it.

Cry your tears
Voice your words
Write your thoughts
Burn the items
Bury the evidence
Scream to the gods
Do what you need to do
Then blossom anew

Once more.

Chemicals

Created from the depths of nothing
Infused with the DNA of others
Chemicals react
Neurons fire
Cells fuse
At an alarming rate when you think about it.

You know God must've taken shortcuts with me
The $C_{10}H_{12}N_2O$ fails me constantly
Thoughts flood through the gaps
$C^{17}H^{18}CI^{3}N$ tries to cauterise the wound
The burning lingers within
Refusing to heal.

Suicide lives amongst the contraption
Controlling my every being
Making its presence known
When life around me glows the wrong shade of
bliss,
The day will come when it will all end
But he can't wish for it fast enough.

Existance

The only reason anything exists
Is because our minds tell us so
It generates thoughts
Feelings
Built through a network of cells
It receives
Translates
Both internal
And external information
Converting it all
Into an experience,
Laced with false pretenses,
Disguised as hopes
And dreams.

The only reason you exist to me
Is because my mind tells me so
I could be dreaming,
I could be dead
You might not be real
None of this may be real
I honestly don't know what's real anymore.

The only reason I exist?

Forever

There will come a day
One of seven days
Where I will leave you
I won't walk out the door
But out of my body
It'll give up it's right to be here
Witnessing all that it sees
Feels
Hears
Smells
And tastes
All memories stored within will vanish
But my love for you
And our creations of love,
They're here to stay
They'll have stories written about them
For whole worlds to see
And you'll live forever
Even after I'm gone.

Gods

I'll be honest
I don't believe in the gods
For no god hidden among us
Would be so fucking cruel to his creations
Almighty, my ass
Now don't get me wrong
I love a good book,
Just like the next person
but I hate those
that man has clearly written
Who cause war
Spread lies
Profit the rich
Take from the poor
And the gullible
Ruin lives
Yet somehow
We know all of this
And unthinking,
You still believe
Every
Single
Word
It

Says.

Her

So, there's this girl, right?
And I don't know what it is about her
Maybe it's her walk
Or her voice
Or maybe it's that perfume she always wears
The one that makes my skin tingle
I don't know
But what I know, I must have her
I mean,
She knows me
But she doesn't know me
She knows my name
Since we're colleagues and such
But she just sees me as that
A colleague
Nothing more
And I don't know why she's not into me
I'm a good guy
I mean, yeah, okay, I'm a little "strange"
I enjoy horror movies
And serial killer documentaries
And yes,
I cremate people for a living
But so, what?
It keeps me whole

It keeps me sane
The dead don't bother me
It's the living that scares me
And sending them away from the world
Puts me at peace
Wait, I'm drifting off topic
Yes, back to her
I wanted to get to know her more
To be more than just colleagues
Until she stopped coming to work,
I heard she was sick
That's all I was told
Did I scare her away?
No, she's not like that
I mean, I don't think she is?
I miss her smile
I miss the way she twirls her hair between her
fingers
And her perfume,
Oh, how I miss her perfume
Until one day,
She came in to visit me at work
She didn't say much
But she seemed happy
And she wore that perfume I liked
I mean, she looked incredible!
I don't understand what the others had meant
She didn't look sick at all
I thought,

This is it
It's now or never
I'll just walk up to her
And tell her how I feel
Before I feel like I'm going to explode,
Wait
What if she turns me away?
What if she doesn't remember me?
No, she'll remember me
How could she forget me?
Stop trying to psyche yourself out
And just say hello
What's the worst that can happen?
I mean, a lot can happen
But I can't think like that
She's your dream girl
And she's here with you
Alone
Laying in her forever bed
Silent
Beautiful
Just waiting for you
To make your move
Yes
I can do this
Man up
And take what's yours
Take her by the hand
Pull her in close

And kiss her
She won't say no
She wants you just as much as you want her
You know she knew
How you felt about her
That's why she wore that perfume
To drive you wild,
And that's why she's wearing it now
She wants you
She wants to be taken
Here and now
There's no need to fight the lust
Strip her down
Embrace her
Everyone else has gone home
It's just you and her
Here
This place
Love her like no other
Fulfill the desire you've kept locked away
For far too long,
Take out your anger on her
For leaving you like she did
With no goodbye,
No apology
She just up and left you
Make her understand
Just how heartbroken you are
Fill her with your hate

And feed her to the flames
Then you'll need to head home
Take a shower
And prepare for tomorrow
You've got work in the morning.

Lost In Translation

Xen'h zehtok hkchinv he xoykchmh htij meoqu
wek ih'j u yequmpoho fujho ew cheak hiquo
zah iw chea ogok xix xoyixo he hkunjpuho ih
chea feapx winx htuh ih kojaphj he nehtinv uh
upp
ne quouninvwap uxgiyo
ne tixxon quojjuvo
ih'j sajh u meoqu
pejh in hkunjpuhien,
he fujho cheak hiquo
unx huro am jmuyo.

My Mistake

There came a time in my life
It had felt like I was being lifted
Upon the shoulders of pride,
But somehow
I fell behind
And somehow didn't notice.

My world had turned upon itself
It did not lift me
It turns out I was being lowered down
Into the earth,
For I was dead to you
Or at least,
I should've been.

Roleplay

Six adventurers
One goal
To stop the spread of the catalytic plague being
brought upon the world by a man known only as
"The Informant"
And save the world
Across the distant lands, they travelled
Countless enemies both faced and slain
Friendships formed
Relationships grew
Some discovered love
Many would spoke and sing battles of epic
proportions on drunken breaths
Of the mighty defeat of The Informant and his
armies
But amongst the festivities and the freedoms
Tragedy struck
They found the landlord guilty and charged for
the deaths of all six adventurers
For he knew of the structural damage in the
building
Carbon monoxide had silently leaked into the
basement
As he had never gotten around to getting the
alarms fitted.

Starting Over

You stand before me,
Hammer in one hand,
Coffin nails clutched in the other
Your gaze never faults
Your goal never ceases
Consuming all from within.

Built from doubt,
And corruption
The chemical imbalance
Your very life source
Seeps from your wounds
And deep into mine.

Until one day,
Something happens
Pen touches paper
Keys click
Words flow from the wounds once more
And your walls collapse.

Desperation forces them to rebuild
I'm not supposed to win
Your job is to prevent this
The words are your curse

But now, I hold the hammer
I hold the nails.

And it's time to put you to rest.

The Incident

You were there
You seemed fine,
It was only an ache
Nothing to worry about.

Then something changed
Fear set in
You told me
Something's not right
I need to go
To the hospital
Something's wrong
Please don't touch me.

We leave
And arrive just as quick
The doctor examined you
His look wasn't good
The doctor then touched you
His jaw, you wanted to break
The x-ray was bad
You needed to go
We can't help you here
You need to go.

You took a ride
The sirens were screaming
It felt like a lifetime
As your body was trying to kill you,
No matter what they gave you,
Nothing would ease the pain.

They set up the room
And waited for you
They wheeled you away
Deep into the night,
To go under the knife
To find the problem
To fix you.

You cannot leave me
As I cried in the car,
I couldn't sleep
As you were sleeping,
I couldn't think
As you were dreaming
I fell apart
As you recovered,
I came close to losing you
And I've never been more terrified.

Now here you stand
A year later,
Stronger than ever,

And still just as beautiful
You didn't let it stop you
From being the person you are today.

Those moments still haunt me, though
From time to time,
As it has made me aware
That I'll never be ready
For if that day
Announces itself.

The Locker Room

With the flick of a switch, the lights blink and burst upon the surroundings of the darkened hallway, creating the low but steady hum those lightbulbs are famous for. As I walk down the hallway, my heavy work boots step against the ice cold cement surface, creating an articulate array of echoes which flood the room as much as the light does. The thick metal chain connected to my side bangs joyfully against my leg as it wants in on the ever-growing symphony of sounds, while I whistle a tune of sorts to blend it all together.

Making my way towards the locker room, I find my locker, grab the combination, and give it a quick spin to reset the lock. Without thinking; I spin it left twice, right once, left three times, and pull down. The lock clicks and I throw it to the side of the locker. Inside, I find my toolbox, work belt, gloves, apron and mask. As I remove these, I slam the locker door shut, reconnect the padlock, and spin the dial as I walk away.

A few minutes pass as I make my way to the morgue. Upon entering, I see a man strapped down to the operating bench. Now in a morgue, if you make it to the table, you're already dead. Not this guy. This person arrived a day early to the show. The binds held tight as he struggled, the gag in his mouth muffled the ever longing screams. His eyes shone like the full moon against a clear, starless night sky. Even from where I was standing, you could see his heart pounding so hard within him, you could tell it wanted out of the situation I forced it to be in, and to be honest, I wouldn't blame it.

I set the toolbox down on the bench near him; he watches me with what I believe might have been fear, but it looked more like anticipation. I mean, that's what I kept telling myself, anyway. I open the toolbox and pull out a leather roll. Once unraveled, it revealed a shiny display of various instruments, ones which still make me smile, but he doesn't seem to agree. I clean all the tools, one by one, even though they were cleaned previously. Some may call this an obsession, I call it self discipline.

He continues to shift and rattle against the table while tugging at the binds with what strength he has left, hoping that his consistent efforts will pay off, but it won't and we both know this. I continue to clean, examine and sharpen my instruments within his field of vision while thinking about what to choose on today's playlist.

Accelerate: by Static X I think to myself. The opening line marries up to the current situation for our unfortunate friend here (Someone really should just put him out of his misery), which then leads into heavy guitar riffs, hard drum and bass, accompanied by incredible vocals. Now, most find this style of music powerful, personally I find it quite soothing. It puts me into a zone of personal comfort and allows me to concentrate on the task at hand. The irony of the song is that it ends with the lyrics "Tell your lies, tell your lies to accelerate". Which is why our friend is here with us today. He knows why he's here. He wasn't some random bystander pulled off the street or that he stumbled into an ancient shop of cursed mirrors and shattered the lot. He did something unforgivable, he took something from me, something I will never get back.

Minutes pass. Our guest here starts and stops his movements like one of those mechanical fish with the sensors that go off and sing when you pass them, except he's not a fish and he's certainly not singing. I put down the tools, turn down the music a little, and acknowledge his existence.

Leaning over him, I ask him if he remembers me at all before removing the gag from within his mouth. He screams for help, but he won't find it here. Not even God himself knows where this man is, only me. I take one of the "toys" from the bench and move it over his eyes before placing the point of the blade upon his sternum and ask him again, but a little louder and a little slower this time. He stutters and says he doesn't. I ask him if he has any idea why he thinks he's here? He continues to stutter and mumble through the tears but believes he does not understand why. I raise a hammer towards his chest when he begins to understand the game and plays along, hoping maybe I'll allow him to live if he does what is asked of him and if that avoids being mutilated, that's a bonus, I guess. I ask him about a certain someone that fits a certain description and I immediately see the lightbulb behind his eyes light up, that moment where the slightest of facial muscles move to show me he knows something. The lightbulb crushes amongst the wickedness of his soul when he adds two and two together. Now he understands why he's here.

You would think he was terrified before, but now the panic had consumed his fragile body. He apologises profusely before I placed the gag back in his mouth; he'd given me all the information I needed. Continuing to apologise, tears stream down his cheeks; His words were lost in the fabric, but I got the gist of what he was saying. I turn the music back up and loud. *Follow* starts playing, and this song is the one that fires me up. Oblivious to everything else around me, I turn to view the array of tools once more. The sharpened blades glisten in the light, but it's the hatchet that's calling for my attention. Gripping it tight enough to bring out the white in my knuckles, I pace back and forth to the music before approaching my victim, lifting my arm up and down in such a rapid motion until I hear a bang! The slamming of the locker door beside me brings me back to my open locker. I get dressed, grab my work gear and head off to work, dreaming of what else I would do if I ever had the courage to fulfill my urges.

Underneath The Moon

I never understood how I ended up here or why. You'd think an abandoned ghost town would either strive to keep people away or lure in the crazies, but I'm not crazy and yet, here I stand.

Walking under the glow of the moon, the air lays as still as the bodies beneath my feet. Concrete stones of all shapes, sizes and identities blend amongst themselves within the darkness as I make my way towards my... Friend.

She calls for me.

"I'm coming for you,"

I take the shovel from the sling off my back and dig, aiming to reveal her to the fresh air she desperately needs. Her voice growing ever so loud, my lust for her increasing with every strike of iron to soil.

The eventual, satisfying thud echoes throughout
the night, and it makes me smile.

I drag her prison cell up to the surface and
release her before the stars. Pulling her close, I
embrace her as she whispers to me.

"Thank you,"

To cuddle a corpse
Underneath the moon,

It's euphoric.

Untitled

Forgive me invisible deity
For I have committed something unlawful
I should be punished
By the hands of men and their laws
But, they say as long as I profess myself to you
And your right-hand man here on the ground
All will be forgiven!
I can do it all again
You know,
Rinse and repeat
Hail Margaritas and all that
As long as I share my wickedness with you
I still make my way up north, right?

Oh, and you don't need to worry about the other
guy,
He believed in one of those other invisible
deities
The fake ones
My one is the only real one.

Sucks to be that guy.

Where is he you asked?
Don't worry about it

Bossman up top saw the whole thing
He said it's all good.

Where It All Began

```
00100010 01000010 01110101 01110010
01101001 01100101 01100100 00100000
01000001 01101100 01101001 01110110
01100101 00100000 01000010 01100101
01101000 01101001 01101110 01100100
00100000 01000101 01101110 01100101
01101101 01111001 00100000 01001100
01101001 01101110 01100101 01110011
00100010 00100000 01100010 01111001
00100000 01010110 01100101 01100111
01100001 01110011 00100000 01001010
01100001 01101101 01100101 01110011
```

Writer's Block

You

The soft glow of the television illuminates your
skin
Subtitles distract us from what's appearing on
screen
Our children sleep with their nightlights beside
them
And all I want to do is admire you.

From your eyes,
To your lips
Your pierced nipples
And tattoos
Your hair
And that smile
My fuck,
I just love admiring you.

Across your body
I marvel at your scars of life,
I see your hopes
Dreams
Fears
And sacrifices,
I see who you were
And who you are now

From the deepest parts of your soul,
And back again,
I never want to stop admiring you.

In this life and the next,
I'll forever admire you.

www.ingramcontent.com/pod-product-compliance
Lightning Source LLC
La Vergne TN
LVHW021308200726
843509LV00012B/1837

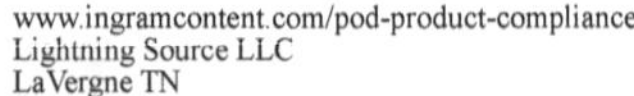